THE SECOND QUESTION

THE SECOND QUESTION

poems by

Diana Der-Hovanessian

The Sheep Meadow Press
Riverdale-on-Hudson, New York

All inquiries and permission requests should be addressed to:
The Sheep Meadow Press
P.O. Box 1345
Riverdale-on-Hudson, NY 10471

Designed and typeset by The Sheep Meadow Press.
Distributed by The University Press of New England.

Printed on acid-free paper in the United States. This book meets the guide-
lines for permanence and durability of the Committee on Production
Guidelines for Book Longevity of the Council on Library Resources.

Library of Congress Cataloging-in-Publication Data

Der Hovanessian, Diana.
The second question : poems / by Diana Der-Hovanessian.
      p. cm.
ISBN 1-931357-45-5 (acid-free paper)
I. Title.

PS3554.E67S43 2007
811'.54--dc22

                                                          2006038219

For my brother Johnny, John Der-Hovanessian, Jr.
You are no longer here; but neither are you not here.

ACKNOWLEDGMENTS

Some of these poems have appeared in the following publications: *AGNI, American Scholar, Ararat, Aurorean, Caduceus, Christian Science Monitor, Classical Outlook, Connecticut Review, Criterion, Entelechy International, Ladies Home Journal, Light, Lyric, Maine Times, McCall's, New York Times, Paris Review, Paterson Literary Review, Southern Review, Wall Street Journal, Worcester Review.*

Some of the poems were published with the following dedications: the title poem *The Second Question* is for Bertha Nakshian Ketchian, *The Art of Making Dances* is for Diana Madden, *How Not to Freeze* for Seta Kalligian and *Horovel* for Hovhanness Badalian.

CONTENTS

SUMMER STREET

THE SECOND QUESTION

LITTLE STORY

OTHER PEOPLE'S STORIES

SUMMER STREET

WHEN SHE LEFT

In Grand Central Station
in the swift moving waves
of commuters, the elastic
waistband of my room-mate's
panties snapped and dropped.

She stepped out of them
without looking down or
looking back, walking head up
indifferent as if the panties
had no connection to her at all

in just the same way she stepped,
a few years later, out of
a sick body and left it lying
there unclaimed, not hers.

WILD MINT

Late April
and I am in the garden
cutting mint
with a small knife,
mint to mix with
oil and lemon
for a salad
you will not share.
Dark April
without you
and I am in the garden
with a knife.
"That plant will take
over your garden if
you let it," my friend
who has followed me outside
advises, "Dig it out."
But its cool
sharp greenness
prods the air with
its pungence, pierces
the last crust of snow.
"Let it," I laugh, "let
it take over my life."

EMILY DICKINSON IN ARIZONA

What do you mean
she never traveled?
Didn't she go to
Washington at twenty three
to visit her congressman
father. That much is
written. That much is clear.

In Philadelphia, on her
return didn't she meet
the distant and "forbidden ear"?
You're right, however.
she stayed home after that year.

We know the rest:
She died in '86.
But in 1890 after her first book
she was seen going west.

LOT'S WIFE

Of course, I looked back.
It was my job to record,
to report. And if I hardened
into a pillar of salt
it was my role to hold up
the past as pillars do.

They also turned to salt
who did not turn to look.
They turned to salt that flowed
and blew away like sand.
They also turned. There was
no either or, only and, and, and.

SPLIT THE LARK

"Split the lark and you will find the music bulb after bulb in silver rolled"
    —Emily Dickinson

There is no music inside
the dead heart, Emily.
No music inside
the ripped harp
and none in yesterday.
Only in flight and song.
Split the lark
and flooding blood
reminds you life
alone is truth.

EMILY BAKING*

It was nourishing
and also prized.
It won a first.
We're not surprised.

As Willa Cather
said "it takes
the same impulse
to make a poem
as bake a cake."

Emily's poems
were unrecognized
but at least
her bread was prized.

* Emily Dickinson won a prize for her bread at the 1897 Cattle Show.

SIX CROWS

Agitated crows with raucous caws
scream in the Harvard Yard. I pause
eating my lunch (at Widener wall,
on a bench near Boylston Hall)
to look up, then down where
they spy a tawny hawk and pigeon prey.

The crows objected, so I thought,
to one of theirs being brought
down as food. "No, no that's not
it." I am told by a student who got
it right. The crows are trying to scare
off the hawk so they can share
the victim lying very dead.
The shouting is about who's fed.

WHAT YOU'LL FIND

You won't recognize
the buildings in
the square.

There's less green,
and more people
everywhere.

Cell phone babblers
have multiplied.

And you've grown
more handsome
since you've died.

AMERICAN ENDING

Father,
old fighter,
never ever
having said yes
to any loss,
you were gentled
at last
in the nursing home
with thorazine
we did not know
was fed you
with the mush.
Over the spoon
that would not stay
inside your grasp
your eyes dripped
fire over
the past.

WIDOW

In an age of arranged marriages
they chose each other. And chose badly.
She first saw him at a picnic.
He was the soldier–hero–speaker.
She was the local beauty, Worcester born,
light haired, soft voiced.
She had put down her kodak. And saw him
pick it up. Or at least she thought
it was hers. But it turned out to be
his own. "Do you want me to show you
how to use it?" she asked trying to
get back her camera. He was amused
as they settled whose was whose.
Later, his cousin who was in love
with her sent him to propose.
But luckily for me, their child,
they married each other instead.
From two distant worlds and mismatched
she ended by hating him until he died.
Then she remembered only the good days,
how handsome he was. How everyone
admired him. And the beginning:
"I was so bold. Like Priscilla Alden
I said, Speak for yourself, John."

FINAL PUNISHMENT

My mother's punishment
for me was the old
silent treatment.
She spoke only to
my sister and brother.
I became invisible.
Mother, mother, look
at me. I am here too.

Now she has gone
punishing us all.
Mother, mother just
say one word. Words
sting such a short time.
Silence forever.

AT THE BAZAAR

At the Book Sale table
you flip open an illustrated
text of saints and gain
a plenary indulgence
from the Queen of Heaven,
divine petitioner
for our redemption.
Next St. Anthony the hermit,
born in Egypt 251 AD looks
startled to be remembered while
St. Isidore patron of gardens
frowns, sending you home
to tend your garden. You turn
one more page to Sebastian
the Roman soldier converted
by Christ on the Cross,
St. Sebastian with arrows
waving in his chest, and you
walk home with his eyes
pin cushioning your flesh.

LITANY

You are the reason for writing
and the lucky poem
I hope to find.

You are the reason for sleeping
and the lucky dream
I want to unwind.

You are the reason for waking,
and the hope that
brings in every daybreak.

You are the pain in my heart and
the salve for every hurt
except that ache.

CONSOLATION

What a soothing word
that attempts, that promises,
what does not exist.

IN THE OLD COUNTRY

The Casa Blanca is rebuilt, renewed
but the same murals stay. The Algiers too,
redesigned, with boys from Beirut replaced
by young men from Yerevan. The Blue
Parrot's flown, like Albiani space
and Bick's of my father's day, gone.

The croissant reigns for a new
generation in Harvard Square.
Musicians fill every doorway
with an exotic island beat while I'm
a stranger at Au Bon Pain where
chessmen play and I understand the phrase
"Old Country" is a time, not place.

WHY I NEVER WAITED FOR PRINCE CHARMING

My grandmother was the blossoming
apricot tree in our backyard
in Marlborough, Massachusetts.
It was planted from a seedling
given to us from one of my
grandfather's old country friends
but grandmother watered it and
showered me with a thousand stories
under its branches, stories
from a faraway land about a king
who had three daughters,
Nazan, Areknazan and Shahnazan,
each princess more beautiful
than the next and all three clever.
All I remember of their adventures
is that whatever happened
Nazan, Areknazan and Shahnazan
always helped each other,
always outsmarted everyone
including any poor prince
who dared come courting. Thank you,
grandmother, of the apricot tree.
Thank you, I guess.

SUMMER STREET, WORCESTER

One, two, or three? I can walk, run,
but don't know the word for balloons.
There they are, – a big bunch tied
with strings to the head harness
of the iceman's horse. I am standing
with the other children in front of
the brick apartment building on
Summer Street where the iceman in a black
leather apron cuts ice he will deliver.
The children are all shouting in English
asking for the balloons. Balloons. That's
what they are. Red. Yellow. Blue. Green
balloons tied to the horse I call "tsee"
in Armenian. As an Armenian kid I know
already it's not nice to ask for anything
no matter how much you want it. Because
your grandmother can read minds
and will give it to you anyway.
The iceman walks toward his horse to
untie the balloons. And the children jump
up and down shouting louder. I watch
wordless, as he takes them all down
and hands them to me! All of them.
Too surprised to say anything to
either the man or children who claw at me,
I run, run down Summer street with
the balloons floating above me. The children
are chasing after. I can't remember more,
not the children stripping away the balloons,
not the little girl who ran. No.
In my mind's eye the balloons hoist her up
and she floats away.

SUMMER SCHOOL

Alba rugosa, white roses,
climb the brick walls while
somewhere a guitar plays
"Ma Rosa, why won't you stay?"

Sprinklers make arcs of rainbows;
girls in thin dresses walk by.
From the dormitory windows
comes "Rosa, don't fly away."

At the cafeteria doorway
a boy pulls white doves from a hat.
They disappear into blue sky.
Everything lasts just one day.

HOW I LOST GOD AT THE MLA CONVENTION

We met at an MLA cocktail
party, God and I.
He wore no name tag and
I asked him why.

—I need no confirmation,
I simply am.

—Oh God, I sighed.

—He nodded, Yes, Ma'am.

—I never believed in you
but hoped you did exist!

—Here I am then, Miss Atheist,
made of thought. And gin.

—No, I corrected, agnostic.
I want to believe. But you have
no halo, just a wicked grin.

Then, before more
words, another woman
latched on to him.

POET

"I hear a dove from other floods"
                        Giuseppe Ungaretti

Not only floods but you
also hear news from
riptides, undertows and
drenching torrents
over lands without

Ararats whose
lofty peaks did not rise
in Noah's time. You hear
speechless unsaved beasts
howling still alive. Other
animals in the blood insisting
now, now write so we survive.

BROKEN NOSE

In the hospital
they set the bone
after removing

all my clothes
and freezing
both sides of my face.

I could not smile
but watched the stain
grow

on the white johnny
black and painless "Oh,
this is how they look

inside
oozing around."
My poems,

dripping
from my broken nose
more gently than ever before.

EPICENTER

"Since I'd never known death before,
I thought it arrived like this with
the spine shaking." Berge Kailian, artist

After the minor earthquake
to show her he cared
her son called my friend Berge
to ask how she fared.

What earthquake? she asked,
I thought the sudden shaking
me awake was my own
final ache.

And don't laugh, she warned,
Sure, no walls caved in.
Everyone feels tremors
first on her own skin.

SHE

She had no mother
to warn her
no experience
no friends

to tell her
to balance
knowledge
and its ends

only a serpent
whispering
only of gain
nothing of loss
nothing of shame
and unlike Adam
she had no one
to blame.

THEY

What made
the marriage last
through lies and snares
was the memory
of the paradise
they once
had shared.

LOVE

"All we call immortal love is in reality—nothing!"
Anna Achmatova

Love is not immortal, Anna.
Nothing lasts.
And the pain of it, Anna,

tell me it too shall pass.

OUR STORY

It was winter, not springtime
You were the spoiled prince
not the knight.

I was the governess, not the princess
but it was time, the right time.

It was a clear winter
without snow
It was a season of ice not harvest
but it was time.

You stamped your feet and demanded
I stood defiant and laughed.
But it was time the right time.

You were the spoiled prince
used to owning.
I was the governess used to governing
but it was the right time our time.

But we let it pass.

FINALLY

His entire life, starting young
he wanted to love someone who
understood his jokes and mother tongue.

Now he is old, he finally does.
He loves the guy that he once was.

EROS

We were invincible
walking tall and young
among the deities
until Cupid's arrow stung.

What did we know
of risk or odds
not knowing only Eros
can wound other gods.

TAKING MY BLOOD PRESSURE

I hear the running
rattle of the thumping heart
as the needle shows
the blood's course and its path,

the fluttering of wings
in sudden flight,
the run of animals
crossing a road at night,

the fin darting in rhythm
to cut the wave's glassy width
diving into the waters
of systolic and diastolic myth

as if the route had no
connection to, no part
with the ear that counts,
the eye that charts.

BLUE LAWS

George Washington en route to
his inauguration in Philadelphia
was stopped midway for
traveling on Sunday.

The blue laws printed on blue
paper banned commerce,
alcohol, and travel on the day
of rest.
          His horses stopped
on the frozen road moved
their blue lips, twitched their tails
and stamped blue stars from
the frozen road.
                 No one measured
how long they had to wait.
No one recorded wind factor
or time. Only that paper
could stop them cold.

REASONS FOR A MARRIAGE

There is no room
for uncertainty.
Duplicate books
are given away.

There is no time
for jealousy.
Laughter settles in
and won't let it stay.

There is finally time
to investigate
the wild creatures
in the closet space.

The left hand
and the right
forgive each
other's mistakes.

THE ASSOCIATED PRESS REPORTS

In spite of critics who fear great harm
will come to Michelangelo's masterpiece,
restorers forge ahead with no qualms

about cleaning David's legs and arms
of decades of grime (with soft chamois
and brushes) in spite of feared harm

that might result in this form
of rubbing. The museum director, not pleased
with earlier restorers had qualms

concerning a Signor Perronchi's balms
rubbed too deeply into David's knees
in spite of others who insist "no harm

comes from mud packs." A storm
of critics cried "Woe!" Among these
an American, J. Beck, warned

against mud. But the director not alarmed
insists "David's not made of nougat candies!
Be calm! A bath every five hundred years
shouldn't cause either howls or qualms.

THE SECOND QUESTION

WHEN GOD WAS A WOMAN

I met her first in the British Museum
and recognized her by her eyes,
duplicates of my twelve year old
daughter's eyes, turned down

at the corners. Armenian eyes
but sculpted perhaps by a fifth century
Greek trained Parthian of
a goddess both cultures shared.

She was labeled, "Anahita, Armenian
goddess," matriarch of a matriarchal
pagan society when goddesses reigned

before Mary replaced them
on altars and before both
were cast aside by invaders.

She was cast in bronze but
called golden mother of
a golden age.

On my second visit to the museum
she was labeled, "Greek Goddess
found in Turkey."

No longer Golden Mother
but tarnished by revisionists
who think mislabeling
can change the past.

FORGIVENESS

Thank you for forgiving for me
my murderer, my rapist, and the thief
of my future, the burner of my house,
the killer of my children, the torturer
of my father. Thank you for your kindness
and your good example.

Thank you for your generosity with my land,
my harvest, my Tigris and Euphrates,
my poplar trees, my wheat fields,
my lilac bushes, my cotton fields,
my Ararat.

Thank you for giving them to the robber
of my youth, the burner of my church,
the executioner of my priest.

Thank you for your open hand and magnanimity
with my goods. I died for Jesus,
I could have denied him and lived.
Forgiveness belongs to him alone.
Let him forgive, if he dares.

THEY SAY: COME HOME

In the plane from Yerevan my seatmates
discuss Armenia. The German physicist says
"I've never seen so many great
scientists in one small place."

The tourist from Ohio replies
"I'm planning to organize
bird watching tours. I was surprised
by the variety, color, size!"

The German gently scoffs, "I don't feel
you'd succeed commercially.
How many birdwatchers could there be?"

I could tell them about the talking birds
that only we the exiled have heard.
But tourists would never believe a word.

THE DELUSION

It was enough it slipped
along the shore, menacing
and dark as the pond.

I didn't care whether my dread
was due to learned fear
or collective taboo.

I was afraid of snakes
no matter what
my grandfather would say

trying to make peace
between me and the lash of
green that whisked over rocks.

He wanted me to see snakes
as pitiful. "See
how this one begs for mercy

rocking back and forth
to spare its life."
Not suspecting

it was poised to strike
had I blocked its escape
I agreed it pleaded

and stepped aside
believing kindness
freed the snake

and made me brave
letting Grandfather
broker both our needs.

40

1915

The Israeli poet says
even Satan has not
invented a revenge
for the death
of a child.

And what poet can
describe the death
of so many children,
so many innocents?

And when there
are not enough
names for sorrow
how can there be
a revenge that
will not cause more?

THE SECOND QUESTION

Where are you,
where were your people from?
was the first question
our grandmothers asked
each other when they met.
The second question
was always How?
How did you escape
death? Now
their children ask
only the first,
where in Turkish Armenia
were your people from?

IN CAMBRIDGE

For no reason that makes
sense to me the sun braids
light with snow
in the mountains.

For no reason I can explain
it is snowing in June
near Kandahar.

For no reason except the season
the light is cracking
like ice.

For no reason I can explain
my brothers and sons
are bombing mountains.

For no reason I can explain
a mountain village
disappears.

I get up and turn on
the light. I get up
and turn the tap

and the water flows.
In Cambridge, Massachusetts
for no reason I know of,
it flows red like blood.

WHAT MY GRANDFATHER TOLD ME ABOUT HELL

God did not invent wars.
He gave his people free will.
God did not invent massacres.
He made men out of clay and
some hardened to stone.

God did not intend Paradise
as the goal but as the land–
scape of beginning.

God did not create Hell.
Fathers do not punish children
like that. His guilty offspring
chose it to expiate guilt.

BRAT

My poor father
with a child like me
who could never sit still
who talked back,
who at 16 thought she

was an expert, telling
him most Armenian

poems were too sentimental
or bloody. Poor Father
whose youth was spent
fighting to avenge
the murder of Armenian
poets (among others),
who went to college in

his twenties, wrote poetry
in three languages,
read it in six, listening
to a brat telling him
what a poem should do
and letting her.

THE FIRST MORNING

in Yerevan you rise and go
to the balcony and watch
in the street below, pagan
goddesses rushing to and fro,
girls of summer. And you want
to shout hello, greetings to you
my lost youth, my homeland sun,
desires once thought tamped and done.
You want to shout, but turn aside
the exile wherever you roam.
"your heart like those ruined houses
of dislodged pillars, broken beams", *
your house always not your home.

* *two lines from an old folk poem, Andouni, for the homeless*

HOROVEL

I am listening
to your tape of Horovel
half song, half yearning
like the Armenian
exile, half alive,
half waiting.
The folk song
calls the oxen,
no the exiled,
with part music,
part tears.

You, who sang
our tears away
born in Baghdad,
lived in Teheran
finally moved
to Yerevan where
you told a taxi
driver once
who had asked
"Yes I'm wealthy.
I have about five
million now."
"Five million rubles,
or dollars?" gasped
the driver. "Yes,
there are five
million Armenians
worldwide. I am rich."

Horovel*
old plowing song recorded by famous tenor Hovaness Badalian who died in 2001

47

FOR LUDA LAUGHING

Your husband asks you to get him
a glass of water and I snap
"Why don't you get it yourself?"
There is a silence.
And I worry that I have gone too far.
But you laugh, Luda, and say to me
as you bring him his water,
"Armenian men think they are pashas."

And your husband turns to say
"She was closer to the water."
"Yes," I say, "in the kitchen
after being at work all day."
I don't say: And probably up all
night to cook the meal
you have invited me to. All night
because the electricity comes
on only at 3 a.m.

The telephone rings and you
are laughing, Luda, with a friend
in the midst of a low running
stream of words I cannot quite hear.

Friends. You will not be my friend
much as I want it. I remain a foreign
associate of your husband, from a country
where electricity and water still run.
You are more interesting, perhaps a better
writer than your husband or me
but my electric machines stand between us.

THE PHYSICS OF BASEBALL

We were sitting at an outdoor café
in Yerevan, a light rain started,
so light it made no sound on
the umbrella overhead. And we
made no move to leave.
The orchestra was playing Vivaldi
when he leaned toward me to ask
for an explanation of the great
American national pastime.

"Television? Or baseball?"

"Start with baseball. What is
a curved ball's curve?"

I stared at him as he reached
for my hand,

"The pitcher's spin, the air
resistance decides the curve's arc,"
I ventured, wondering how much
of my English he understood,

Speaking in Armenian he reminded
me gravity decides
the pull toward earth.

"Is this some sort of
physics test?" I laughed,

"What about the batter's skill?
What about timing? Isn't your
baseball more about timing
than our football?"

"What are we talking about?"
"Mostly about the great international
game, love," he said.

WILD DOGS

Unowned strays howled all night,
that year in Yerevan. Unnamed
mongrels yowled each morning
behind my dormitory in the empty
lot where construction workers
piled up bags of refuse.

Every morning I was wakened
by barking at first light.
Where did they come from,
these wild dogs? Did they breed
from dogs no one could afford
to feed?

One day it was quiet.
One morning there was no sound
when I looked from my window.
Then I saw why the dogs
had abandoned the empty yard
...a huge, tawny cat, the color
of cinnamon clay, shaped like
a leopard, was ferreting
in the trash. Quite alone.

"You dreamed that cat," some friends
laughed when I described the visitor.
But a poet confirmed it was "a Siberian
tiger, sometimes seen this far south.
A hungry cat scatters every other beast."

SAFFRON TEA

Alexander at Persepolis for a year
tasted saffron for the first time (in his rice)
cooked Persian style with the golden spice.

He saw how crocus stamens in the fields
were plucked to use for flavoring and dyes
at sunrise when workers would rise

in autumn at the second blooming of the flowers,
saw how purple blossoms yield in threes,
triple filaments that were cut and dried.

In Persepolis even hair could acquire gold light
with it, or one could, like Cleopatra use
saffron for bathing, if not in kitchen stews.

Alexander's men took it westward from the east,
to flavor pilavs back in Greece.

From there Italians, Spaniards, Portuguese

grew their own, where ounce for ounce
it was worth its weight in gold
even now as in the days of old.

And if you brew it for your morning tea,
it's said, in your cup you'll see
dawn rising from the Caspian Sea.

VEHICLE IN VINES

Breton's
auto–
matic writing
stopped
this car
then backed
it up
out of the
vines
into this dream
pistons idling
car rocking
silently
I fix it
with a lover's
stare
at the gear
box
men love
their cars
when
they're
in vines
a paradox
like loving
you from this
distance

THREE A.M. DREAM

You: I feel apart, a stranger, homesick for some far-off Armenia I have never seen. A remote village..."

But meanwhile you wake into
foreign air that will pale
your skin and you will talk
with facile slang you have acquired
like currency to exchange
for smiles and new jokes.

In your sleep you keep that other
country called vague unhappiness,
an alienation you call home.

You lock the gates so
no one else can immigrate
calling it America.

You people it from the inside
with a dream two hundred, no,
two thousand years old.

In the dream four laughing children
sit in a wagon drawn by oxen.
They are yours and they also
belong to that me who died long ago.

In your dream I say: Go. Go.
But still you linger as if
it would be a crime to abandon us.
You turn in your sleep guiltily
reaching for something forgotten
yet not gone.

In the morning you will dress
and walk through a glazed city
toward your smiling future
with a frown.

LETTER FROM ROUPEN SEVAG*

They take me to my new patient. On the way
From my prison I pass the cell where
I see Varoujan writing every day.

My patient is improving perhaps by May
she will no longer need my care.
Like Varoujan I write every day

but to you. What will happen we cannot say.
I doubt if there will be trials. There
is only patience for us now. I pray

for you and the children. Please relay
my love to them and friends if they're
safe. Varoujan and I nod every day

as we pass. We're not allowed to stay
or talk. As for the others I'm unaware
of where they were taken on the way

from the April round-up. Go stay
with your parents. I will always
love you. Be patient. Just the way
Varoujan keeps writing every day.

*Varoujan and Sevag were among the 250 Armenian writers rounded up on April 24, 1915 at the onset of the Turkish genocide of the Armenians. Sevag, a physician, was offered his freedom if he would forsake his Christianity and family and marry his Turkish patient. He refused and was executed with Varoujan and the others. Varoujan's prison poems were ransomed by a jailer to an Armenian priest and published five years later in the diaspora under the title SONGS OF BREAD.

WHEN I GO BACK TO HAYASDAN

When I go back to Hayasdan
I will take my mother.
She will no longer dread
the Communists and what
they have done to the country
she has never seen.
We will find my father in
the mountains of Karabagh.
He will run to greet us
shouting, Didn't I tell you?
Didn't I tell you how
beautiful it is?

No, I will say, you did not.
You never told me anything.
I had to see for myself.
I had to read your book
to know how you fought
in these hills. I had to find
you after you died.

When I go back to Armenia
it will be in the time
of apricots and pear blossoms.
And when the cranes return
bringing all the exiles
who ache for home.

No, it will be in summer, Vartavar,
the pagan feast celebrated
as Resurrection Day.
When I go home to Armenia
it will be Vartavar and summer

when the naughty boys of Yerevan
throw water at all passing girls
in summer dresses.
Perhaps I will see you and
and you will sing "Kele, kele."

No I will be alone and remembering
that day in 1981 in the lobby of
Hotel Armenia when I burst into
tears seeing a small woman
the duplicate of my grandmother,
wanting so much to hold her,
hear her voice but she was not
my grandmother. The writer with
me took my hand and led me to her.
    When I go back to Armenia
    it will be my grandmother.

THE ARTSAKH SOLDIER TO HIS WIDOW

If I gave my life for Artsakh
let Artsakh be my gift to you.
Don't mourn, don't mourn, my darling,
but live enough for two.
I do not say forget me.
I do not say forgive.
But don't wear black, my darling,
just live, just live, just live.

BY NOW

By now we should have finished grieving.
By now we should have reached some peace.

By now there should have been atonement,
and the pain slightly eased.

By now witnesses are almost gone.
And the lies about our bones believed.

By now they thought we'd be forgotten
and our blood dried to dust and gone.

By now they thought our books and churches
would topple into ash and stone.

By now they thought our stolen children
would have all turned into Turks.

By now they thought aid money
sent back to America would do its work

in changing history's truth to lies:
that we were never here alive.

By now they thought the last survivors
and their children would be in graves.

They didn't count on our children's children
being even angrier and more outraged.

HOW NOT TO FREEZE

I can help you feel warmer,
says Seta as we run from
our cars into icy wind.
How?
Once frost bitten, always cold
I want to say, shivering.

It's truly a matter
of not expecting
not admitting, not saying,
you are cold, she continues,
as I stare at her laughing,
in a light jacket,
glowing under the secret
Syrian sun that follows her.

PARADISE

"I turned down a job in Paradise, Florida.
How many Armenians could there be there?
I'd find more in Siberia." overheard in Kay's Market

Give me Alaska
with its stark
wolf-tooth weather,

the Congo swamp,
the dankest city
danger

where asphalt
melts; the barbed
wire camp to bear

or curse; forests
under Grendel's
spell,

the darkest ages,
the netherworld,
or any hell

rather than paradise
shared only
with a stranger.

WAR IN IRAQ

Sinbad the Sailor
and the huge flying roc
and all the genies
of your childhood
lived in Baghdad.
Your geography book Ur
and your history book
Mesopotamia,
your bible Babylon,
the Ziggurat Temple
of the moon and
the Abbasid Palace
of the sun...
all the genies
of your childhood
are out of their
bottles now.

THE ARMENIAN SPEAKS

I

Hey, am I the only one left
to speak for my old
enemy, the Assyrian?
Am I the only one left
to cry out, "you mean
Assyrian, Sumerian!"

Am I the only one left
to remember Nineveh,
Babylon and Ur
from the old days?

The only one left
to say, "Hey, Baghdad
is older than Ottomans,
older than Arabs.
What a short memory
you newsmen have!"

II

The Euphrates
red with Armenian
blood, blue
with the ink of
stolen books cast
into its waters,
the Euphrates
that defined

the Garden of Eden
glistens now with
Arabic, Kurdish,
Turkish, American
lust for oil.

WHY HE FLED

You on that bicycle in 1994
rushing at me crossing
Quincy with the stream
of pedestrians, why did
you knock over only me?
You who stood wringing your hands
apologizing when I woke surrounded
by kneeling men and a nurse
telling me not to move, saying
I had broken my neck. Telling me
the ambulance was here and I
would be taken to the hospital.
"No" I said leaping up. "My neck
cannot be broken. My mother
is waiting. I have to go home."
Then the emergency men gripped
me into the gurney tying me down
while I pleaded No, and you, my death,
kept repeating "Forgive me, I was
going too fast." You looked so
startled as I handed you back a
a blood soaked handkerchief saying
"Don't worry" while the ambulance
men not knowing my skull was cracked
strapped me back while I pleaded
to be free but you, Mr. Death,
seeing the kneeling people, fled.

ENDING WITH FROST

*"Some say the world will be overrun with viruses; others say cockroaches.
But I say crows." Ask The Globe column*

Some say roaches will
overrun the globe.
Others rule viruses
will deal the final blows.
From what I'd seen
of pettiness, I supposed
the roach theory best.
But now listening to
TV's raucous prose.
I hold with those
who favor crows.

SUPERVIVIENTES

Survivors
those of us who
live beyond
live over
live after
live through
live past
who walk over
the cracked earth
walk out of
walk free
not superior
not super human
not supermen
but blessed,
cursed to be
the future
of our dead.

THE ART OF MAKING DANCES

If music is time in motion,
if the stage is space defined,
then dance is their wordless story.

Let it entertain the eye.
Let it aim at the solar plexus.
Let it throb with the heart.

Let it march through the orient
and the ballet schools of Europe
to leap leap leap,

making its music concrete
to sweep like a wind
that lifts everyone with it.

MIST

The sea is gone and the sky is gone
    and yet
the cliffs are gray and the sand is gray
    and wet
where the sea once reached and the sky once reached
    and met.

SHOWING OUR AGE

"The New World is no longer new"
                    Robert Hughes, art historian

The Puritan contract has been broken,
marketing has won at last.
Do–it–yourself is now do–it–by–computer.
The Ash Can School is in the trash.
Thinking is no longer a priori;
materialism no more austere.
Benjamin West is forgotten.
The Academy of the New no longer here.
Frank Lloyd Wright is not the pivot.
High Fashion is no longer king.
Even Sensuality and Pleasure need
excessive adjectives to zing.
Criticism is in the hand of cynics.
The Puritan Contract is torn.
Emerson and Thoreau are
social writers, not poets.
Silk top hats are no longer worn.

COLD FIRE

A fire once it's dead stays dead
in women. But in most men
cold fires can revive and spread

again; the closed book opened and re-read.
A woman's a different specimen.
Her fires, once they're cold stay dead.

All that is let go or shed
stays shed, not played out again.
Men's ashes can be relit to spread.

A woman wants a fire. That's bred
into her bones, but when
the fire is dead it's really dead,

the love discredited stays dread-
ed. But dead dreams in men
sleep in banked fires that can spread.

A man's old yen can be retread-
ed. But women, once they say amen
let old flames remain cold and dead.
Men's fires recombust, it's said.

72

SEVEN WARNINGS
IN SEARCH OF AN ARMENIAN FEMINIST
(for Erica Jong)

Beware of the man who closes his eyes when he kisses.
    He's kissing someone else.

Beware the man who over-praises your cooking.
    He's going to invite his friends over.

Beware the man who brags about his gourmet cooking.
    You can never please him.

Beware the man whose closets have more clothes than yours.
    He's interested more in his own body.

Beware the man who tells you how to cook.
    He's going to move in his family from Beirut.

Beware the man who doesn't like your poetry but
    asks you to write his reports.

Beware the man who spends hours buying shoes.
    He's going to walk all over you.

LITTLE STORY

LITTLE STORY

In your arms,
half asleep
your breath on my cheek;
in your arms
you asleep
everything complete;
in your sleep
the name you speak
is Ani. I am Marguerite.

POST PARTY BLUES

After a party most people
climb into bed
thinking of witty things
they wish they had said.

Not me. Such regrets
never disturb my repose.
I just wish I had kept
my mouth firmly closed.

SEXIST POEM

Poems have neither sex nor age.
The true poet's praise and rage
are genderless upon the page,
difficult to identify
except by a woman's eye.

COLUMBUS

Columbus would never
have left Palos City
if he waited approval
from a committee.

78

UNINVITED

She didn't believe in paradise
and so it was a shock
to see its shining towers rise
and find them barred and locked.

THE POLISHED ONE

The rolling stone
gathers no moss
but accumulates
its share of gloss.

CANDIDATE'S MATE

Standing beside every man called great
is the brave woman, sure as fate,
who can remind him, face to face,
of his truly proper place.

FAULTS WITNESS

To ferret out your secret faults
don't run to analyst or pastor,
run for office and you'll learn
what's wrong with you much faster.

WOMEN'S RIB

Man might have been a lot wiser
if Eve came first as supervisor.

LOVE POTION

To win a heart
takes less beauty than wit.
But it helps to look like
his mother a bit.

BAD PRESS

Why do we scream
when mice skitter over rugs?
They're tiny mammals
we see huge bugs.

HONEST FACE

Not every woman hides her age.
There are honest ones you know
like me who don't deny their years
because they just plain show.

NON VOYAGE

Miss the pristine painted dapple
of the papal Sistine chapel?
Miss the current bistro list
where Existentialists exist?
Miss pyramids and Pyrenees
and peering at Bavarian knees?
Miss China trade and trying out
Brussels sprout and Guinness stout?
Don't feel left upon the shelf.
Just congratulate yourself.
This year's foreign trip not made
is your bit for balanced trade.

PATIENCE, FRIENDS

They grow their hair
when you want it trimmed,
cut it when long looks great,
leave school when you want them in,
go back when you think it's late,
marry much too soon and then
come home when you want them gone.
Children eventually do
everything you wanted done.

BALANCING ACT

Checkbook errors make us
sad, then glad
when we prove it is
friend husband who can't add.

ICARUS

"The bat is the only mammal
capable of flight." dictionary
definition

After Daedalus taught him how to fly
he floated up like a lark
into the sun's hot searing eye
forgetting bats flew in the dark.

CRUISE BLUES

Girls who trip
around in pairs
seldom get
much past the stares.

DON JUAN

Green, green kindling
was what he sought

snapping, splintering
and then he forgot

to watch it burn
when the bonfire caught.

ON COMMON GROUND

Marriages made in heaven
once they get to earth
are exactly like all matches
of less celestial birth.

ROCK AGES

Ex-jitterbugs have children,
it's a good bet,
who think mom and daddy
did the minuet.

EARNING A REST

The trouble with making a list
comes when the list's complete.
I think, by writing down each job,
I've done something concrete.

ALIVE AND WELL

That fat faced girl I hated all these years
'though now I'm slim and worldly wise,
smiles from the class reunion screen
evoking cheers and sighs. Surprise!
Hey. She's gone. Look who's here,
sophisticated, even avant-garde.
But blind classmates keep her in their eyes
not me. And wasn't she a card?

NATURE'S PLAN

Children who spoke
softly, sweetly,
wake up one day
changed completely,

teenage boors,
with the house shaking,
making letting go
less heart breaking.

LOVE LIKE A ROSE

Love like a rose
will bud, blossom and climb.
But love at first sight
saves lots of time.

AFTER BEN FRANKLIN

Early to bed
early to rise
prevents those puffy
t.v. eyes.

OUT OF HIS ABSENCE

she has stoked
passions
he could not evoke.

Out of his absence
she's devised an idol
only he could recognize.

FOREIGN IMPRESSIONS

Our tour of Europe
left us dismayed
The Joneses saw us
at the worst place we stayed.

EARMARK

In spite of dangles
hoops and spheres
men seldom notice
girls have ears.

DOWN HILL

I love to come on sights like these:
crystal leaves on silver trees.
Unless they come between my skis.

DO YOUR PANTYHOSE GIVE YOU A FIT?

Figuring out charts
of weight and size
is existential exercise.

HECKLER

The heckler
at the poetry reading
interrupts me with a whine.

Why don't you? she advises,
her epiphanies
climaxing mine.

Madam, I'm not always "I",
I say, I just write
the stuff.

Hmmph, she says loudly,
that's bad enough.

CAUCASIAN PROVERB

The early bird that caught the worm
will soon be feeling quite infirm.
In spite of being fed and fat,
chances are he woke the cat.

SOME SHARING

He kept house and bachelor table
without complaint or quaver.
But now any housework's labeled
doing her a favor.

SIX DECENT LINES

Six decent lines can make a man immortal,
said Ezra Pound. But what if knocking at the portal,
no one hears, let alone answers his six pleas
except for dogs and children? No one lets him in.
And all he gets for his metric similes
are bruised knuckles and a bitten shin.

THE FALSE PRINCE REPLIES

And so he turned and left
Had he but knelt and laid his lips on hers
he would have been the prince.   C.A. Trypanis

The trouble with waking Sleeping Beauty was
waking the others, king, cook, chicken boys.
I hated noise.

The trouble with waking Sleeping Beauty was
timing. My knee would not bend.

If she had opened up her eyes
the dark would end.
The trouble was

beyond the gate
the path led back to dendrite roads and
I had learned too well to hesitate.

CIRCUS CAREER

Nico swinging through the trees
plans a life on the trapeze.
"Also teacher," adds Uncle John,
"something to fall back upon."

TOP JOBS

The only inventor
I'd like to throttle
is the one who perfected
the child proof bottle.

When you're sick with flu,
or weak with grippe
you have to call a kid
to pry off its lid.

IN WHICH A MUSE IS COMPARED
TO A BIRDFEEDER AND WARNED
HE WON'T GO FREE

These are not the sort of seeds
I had in mind, Mr. Muse,

but you are very kind
and I thank you.

However, haven't you read somewhere
that affection grows

deeper in the feeder
than in those fed? Take care.

Look at keepers of pets everywhere.
Look at poor Mother. Beware.

WESTERN WOMAN

The troubadour
who propped her up
on a pedestal
and on a shelf
forbade you
to look up her dress
although that angle
made it easiest.

Then came the man
with Judo–
Christian tracts
when she complained
who sent her
off to Saks.

FOR MY INCOMPATIBLE LOVE

You can praise the morning light
and I the evening skies.
When shadows stir the mourning dove
to humming as you rise
while steeples swim out of the dark
I will not do likewise.
You may write aubades for day,
I'll stick to lullabies.

OTHER PEOPLE'S STORIES

Translations and Adaptions

AFTER CATULLUS

Like a dumb fish suffering
all this love and hate,
I am hooked and flopping
yet still panting for the bait.

WE NEVER DISCUSS TRAPPING MONKEYS

You know how it's done, of course,
with bottles and sugar. The monkey thrusts
in a paw and can't extricate
his fist without giving up his bait
and won't. He's captured thus.
But why should monkeys concern us?

Translated from Kevork Emin

GANGSTER'S FUNERAL

Harmless at last
he lies in state,
finally dignified,

like the snake
going straight
only after it died.

Translated from Kevork Emin

ON FIRST LOOKING AT A PAPERBACK HOMER
with bows to Keats' "On First Looking Into Chapman's Homer"

Much have I traveled, not by choice but sent,
and the good states of our republic have seen.
Numberless the times, in thrall have I been
held up at airports by storm or travel agent
whims. When with books shipped ahead, so often
I searched reading, in racks and magazines,
all with covers of scant clad teens,
books in need of wrapping up again.

But finding Homer, pursued by naked women,
I decide, he for one would not be surprised
to be shown in dark glasses, little else, even
to be carried (in English) through the skies,
over the mountains, valleys, over Darien,
more at ease than I am, as time flies.

VILLANELLE FOR VILLON

Unrestricted acquaintance is sure to lead to disgust with his (Villon's)
revolting realism and rascality.

Chamber's 1908 Biographical Dictionary

Where are the ladies nowadays
to say nothing of gentlemen, so unaware.
Where are the snows of yesterday?

Where are the prim readers who dare say
unrestricted Villon is unfit fare?
Where are the ladies nowadays

with delicate cheeks ready to blaze
at the rascality should a rascal swear?
Where are the snows of yesterday?

Poets of either sex would amaze
poor Villon. He'd up and declare
where are the ladies nowadays

who faint away inside bone-stays,
who write in lilac ink and care
where the snows are of yesterday?

Where is such realism that dismays
with rascality? Vin-ordinaire.
Where are the ladies nowadays,
and the snows of yesterday?

OBITUARY LIST

He scans
the list
with mount–
ing dread.

Then sighs;
he's not among
the dead.

Adapted from Zahrad

After William Wordsworth's sonnet LONDON 1802

NEW YORK, LONDON 1902

Emily Post! We need you in this age
of violence. New York and London must learn
the thoughtful way to picket, hi-jack and burn
for causes without rancor, without rage.

Where are you? The proper spoon and cup
for coke seems unimportant but grace
might add solace as the human race
prepares politely to blow itself up.

Emily Post, thy soul was like a star.
Thy voice, calming as the deep sea
settling common drifters free
by instructing how to address the far-
off nobility. Now, in times so dark
we need your sea, your joyous bark.

RIVALS

Whenever I see her
I weigh the old pain.
Or was I lucky to lose him?
How much did she gain?

I remember my hurt
and terrible grieving.
Then I weigh her fate
and we come out quite even.

from an Armenian poem by Medakse

FOR SOMEONE TURNED TREACHEROUS

It's not your treachery,
or your gossip I mind.
Your stab in the back,
your pettiness, I find
rather amusing.
But puzzling. I rack
my brain trying to find
good reasons: but
you are no relative of mine,
neither son, nor love,
nor anyone I saved,
and not the person
I gladly gave
my last piece of bread.
So, why this hostility?
I really don't know.
What is the great favor
you think you owe?

from Kevork Emin

PRAISE TO THE SULTAN

We can never forget you, great sultan.
You have earned eternal fame
by filling every calendar blank
with a new martyr's name.

Adapted from Raphael Patkanian

BALLADE DES DAMES DU TEMPS JADIS

"ou sont les neiges d'antan"

by Francois Villon

Tell me to what distant place
Did Wallis Simpson go?
Where is Louise Brooks whose face
launched a thousand echoes
Of clipping shears? Do let me know
By what shore Veronica Lake
Stands with beauty real or fake?
And where are last year's, past years' snows?

Where's Amy Lowell with her cigars?
Where did Amelia Earhart fly?
Akhmatova, whose son behind bars
Made her write and made us cry?
Anna Pavlova, and Melba, toast
Of three continents, rows on rows,
Madga Lupescu, whose hair was most-
Ly flame. Where are last year's melted snows?

Where's Mata Hari? Where's Margaret Meade
For whom New Guinea came of age?
Marion Davies, movie lead
Who made Hearst into her page?
Where is divine Sarah now on stage?
With Janis Joplin, and Tokyo Rose,
Josephine Baker, Parisian rage?
And where are the past and last year's snows?

Do not ask Prince or Michael J.
Not even the queen of the airwaves knows,
Not even Barbara Walters will say
Where are the past and last year's snows.

PUBLICATIONS BY DIANA DER-HOVANESSIAN

Books of Poetry

The Second Question, Sheep Meadow Press, Riverdale, N.Y.
The Burning Glass, Sheep Meadow Press, Riverdale, N.Y.
Any Day Now, Sheep Meadow Press, Riverdale, N.Y.
    winner of the Paterson Prize
The Circle Dancers, Sheep Meadow Press, Riverdale ,N.Y.
Selected Poems, Sheep Meadow Press, Riverdale, N.Y.
About Time, Ashod Press, N.Y.
Songs of Bread, Songs of Salt, Ashod Press, N.Y.
How to Choose Your Past, Ararat Press, N.Y.

******

Books In Armenian

Recycling Day, Armenian Writers Union Press
Valley of Flowers, Nayirie Press
Inside Green Eyes, Black Eyes, Sovet Press Yerevan

Translations

Anthology of Armenian Poetry, Columbia U. Press, N.Y.
    winner of P.E.N/ Columbia and Kolligian Awards
Land of Fire, Selected Poems of Eghishe Charents, Ardis Press Ann Arbor
    Mich. winner of Vande Bovenkamp and Arrmand Erpf
    Awards for excellence in literary translation
Sacred Wrath, Poems of Vahan Tekeyan, Ashod Press N.Y.
The Arc, Selected Poems of Shen Ma, St. Vartan Press, N.Y.
    (the above four edited with M. Margossian, translated by DDH)
The Other Voice, Armenian Women's Poetry, edited with Maro Dalley
    AIWA Press, Watertown, MA

Coming to Terms, Selected Poems of Vahan Derian, Ashod Press, N.Y.
Selected Poems of Gevorg Emin, International Poetry Forum Press
For You On New Year's Day, (Gevorg Emin) Ohio University Press,
     Athens, Ohio
Across Bucharest After Rain, Selected Poems of Maria Banus, Quarterly
     Review of Literature, Princeton N.J. Winner of QRL prize
St. Grigor Narekatsi, with Thomas Samuelian, VEM Press, Yerevan,
     Armenia

AUTHOR BIO

New England born poet Diana Der-Hovanessian was Fulbright Professor of American Poetry at Yerevan State University in 1994 and 1999. She is the author of 22 books of poetry and translations and has awards from the National Endowment For the Arts, Poetry Society of America, P.E.N. Columbia Translation Center, Paterson Poetry Center, P.E.N. New England, Armenian Writers Union, Writers Union of America, *Prairie Schooner* and *American Scholar.* She has been a long time poet-in-the-Massachusetts Schools and has led translation and poetry workshops and taught poetry of human rights in universities here and abroad. She is president of New England Poetry Club.